HEADING SOUTHWEST

Along the Santa Fe Trail

An Activity Book for Children

Written and illustrated by William E. & Jan C. Hill

© Copyright HillHouse, 1993

Second printing, 1998

ISBN 0-9636071-1-1

1

HEADING SOUTHWEST

The city of Santa Fe was founded by the Spanish many years ago before the United States existed. Early trappers and traders heard exciting stories about Santa Fe. They soon decided they wanted to go there to trade. The first successful American trader was William Becknell. In 1821 he went to Santa Fe and later returned to the United States. Soon other traders followed and trade with Santa Fe began.

The trail to Santa Fe was about one thousand miles long. The beginning of the journey was across the prairie or grasslands and along rivers. Then the trail divided. One branch went across a desert or long hot, dry area. The other branch had to climb over high rugged mountains. Soon both branches of the trail joined together. Just before reaching Santa Fe the trail crossed over some more mountains. Once in Santa Fe the traders celebrated and sold their trade goods. The traders bought some Mexican trade items to sell back home. Then they started on their way back.

At first most of the people who traveled over the Santa Fe Trail were traders or merchants. They traveled in groups called caravans. The men who drove the wagons and animals were called teamsters. Soon pioneer families with children traveled to Santa Fe. The traders used big heavy wagons to carry all their trade goods. The pioneers also used wagons, but their wagons were usually smaller than the traders' wagons.

The traders and pioneers usually traveled only about fifteen to twenty miles a day. Some days they would only travel a few miles, because of problems such as wagon breakdowns or difficult river crossings. The journey would take almost two months of walking.

During the 1860s construction on the railroad began. In 1880 the railroad was completed to Santa Fe. Most people and goods then moved by train. This greatly reduced the use of the Santa Fe Trail. Within a few years it was almost forgotten.

There is a map in the middle of the book. It shows the locations of some of the forts and sights that the traders and pioneers saw. Many of the travelers started at Independence, Missouri. Some started at other towns along the Missouri River. Then the trail headed southwest towards Santa Fe. When the first traders and pioneers went to Santa Fe it was part of Mexico, but today it is part of the United States.

As you read through this book you will learn many things about the Santa Fe Trail and the people who traveled along it. You will see some of the sights they saw. You will learn about some of the people who went and what goods they brought along with them. There are also some fun activities and puzzles to do. There is even a fort to build. We hope you enjoy the exercises and get them done correctly!

Good Luck!!!

Jan & Bill

A long time ago traders, or merchants as they were also called, traveled southwest to Santa Fe to sell their goods.

William Becknell opened the trail to Santa Fe in 1821. He started from a place near Franklin, Missouri. He returned in 1822. Within a few years most of the traders began their journey to Santa Fe from a town called Independence, Missouri. Here is the old Independence Courthouse in the square from which the traders left for Santa Fe.

One of the places in eastern Kansas where the traders and pioneers stopped was Council Grove. It was a good place to camp and rest because it had lots of woods and cool running water. In a grove of trees by the river representatives of the American government signed a treaty with the Indians who lived in the area. It allowed the traders to travel safely through Indian lands.

4

Land formations, or landmarks, were frequently used by travelers to guide them along the trail. Several of them are shown on some of the next few pages.

Pawnee Rock was a famous landmark on the trail in Kansas. The land around it is very flat and grassy and is called a prairie. From a distance some travelers thought that Pawnee Rock looked like a wart sticking up out of the flat prairie. Travelers often saw buffalo in the area.

Bent's Fort was one of the most important resting stops on the trail. Here the travelers and traders could buy additional supplies, get needed help, or trade with the Indians. The fort was located on the banks of the Arkansas River in eastern Colorado. It was made out of sun-dried mud bricks called adobe. During the early years it was the only fort on the trail. Today it has been reconstructed and is open to visitors.

The Spanish Peaks were two well-known mountains in southeastern Colorado. Travelers could first see the Spanish Peaks a few days after leaving Bent's Fort. They could see the peaks for two weeks during their journey. The antelope was another animal often seen on the trail.

Another famous landmark is called Round Mound. It is located on the branch of the trail in northeastern New Mexico. Here is the scout leading the wagon caravan. Many travelers climbed the mound to get a good view of the area.

Here is the most famous landmark on the trail. At first some traders thought it looked like a shoe. Later other traders thought it looked like a wagon with oxen heading towards Santa Fe. Which do you think it looks like?

Most traders finally agreed that it looked like a wagon. They named it Wagon Mound.

Draw your own wagon on the trail.

This is the town square in Santa Fe. It is in the center of the city. The cathedral is in the background. Around the square the traders sold their goods in shops. Even today, people buy and sell goods in shops and on the sidewalks around the square.

10

What does the numbered secret message say? It could have been a headline from a newspaper printed in January, 1822. Use the decoder at the bottom. Write the letter for each number in the space below the number. What does the secret message say?

_____

ST. LOUIS MONTHLY NEWSPAPER
January, 1822

8   6   11   10   3   10   6

___ ___ ___ ___ ___   ___ ___

9   1   5   10   1   4   3   6   7   3   5   3   2

___ ___ ___ ___ ___   ___ ___   ___ ___ ___ ___ ___ ___ !

1	2	3	4	5	6	7	8	9	10	11
A	D	E	F	N	O	P	R	S	T	U

11

Traders saw or used many animals. Complete the pictures and name them. Write their names in the spaces below the drawing.

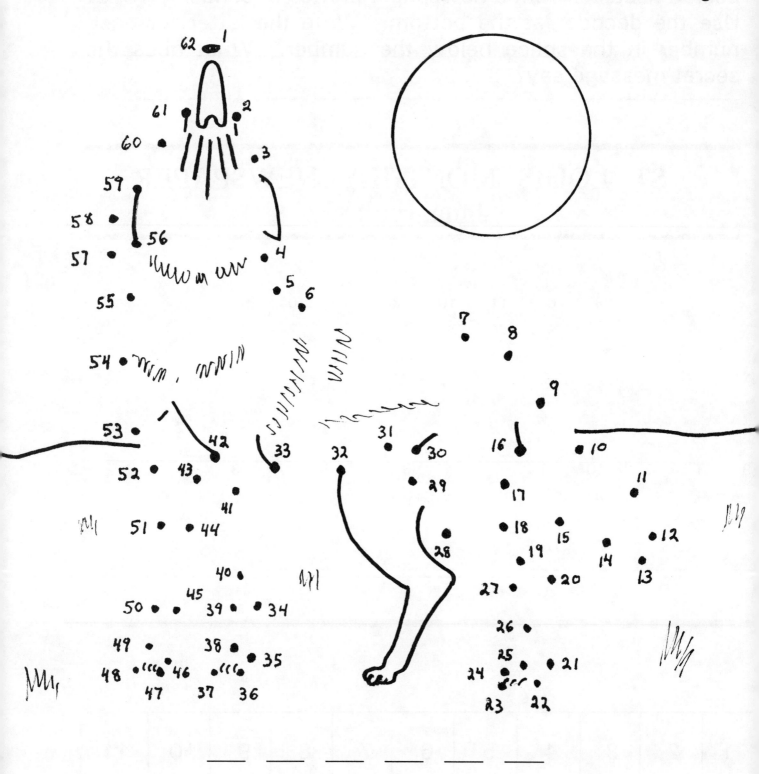

This animal was often seen by the traders and pioneers. Usually it was seen from a distance. It could often be heard howling at night. Some people called it the "song dog." Do you know what it is?

This animal is rarely seen today except in zoos or in a few national parks. However, early travelers wrote about seeing it along the trail. It is brown in color and is one of the largest animals in North America. What is it?

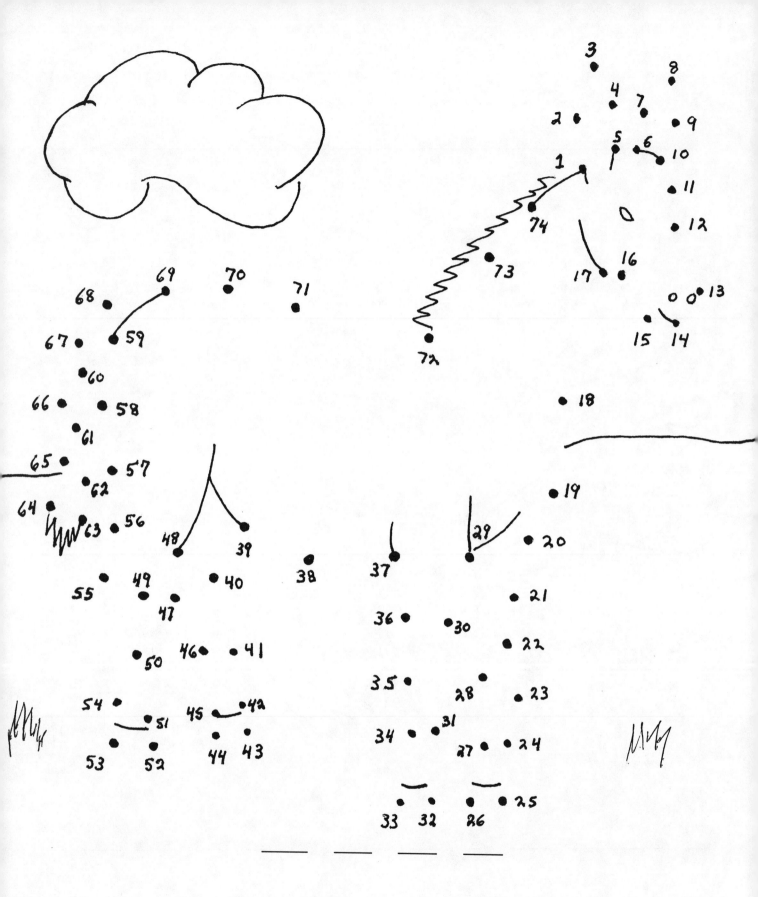

Traders brought this animal to Missouri from Santa Fe. Missouri soon became famous for it. People thought it could be very stubborn. Some traders used several of them to pull their wagons. What animal is it?

Color the items that the traders and pioneers could have heard while traveling on the Santa Fe Trail.

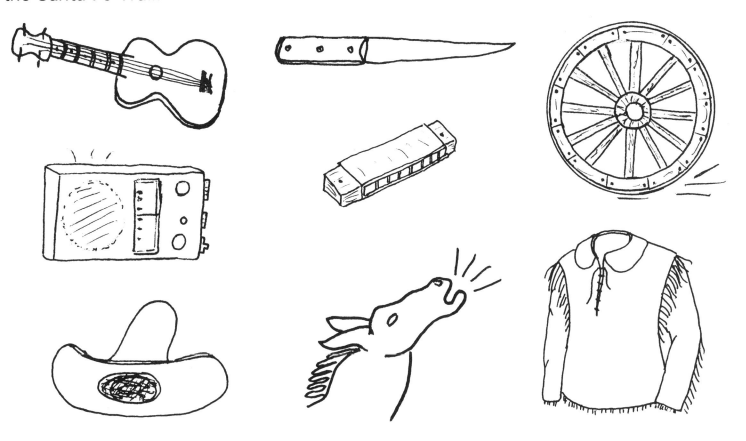

Color the items that the traders and pioneers could have smelled while traveling on the Santa Fe Trail.

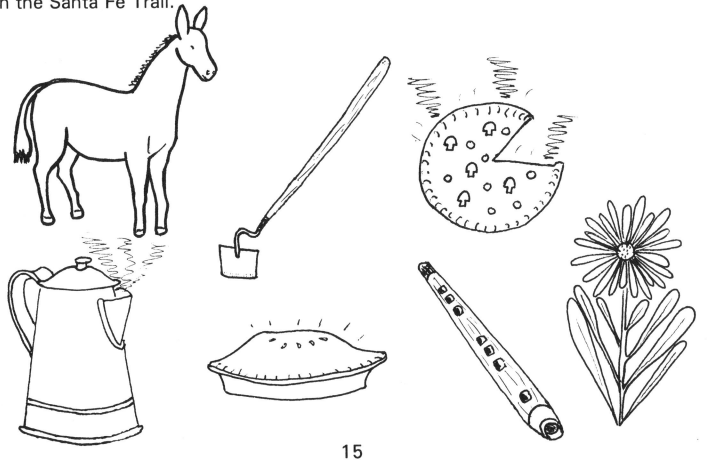

MAP OF THE SANTA FE TRAIL

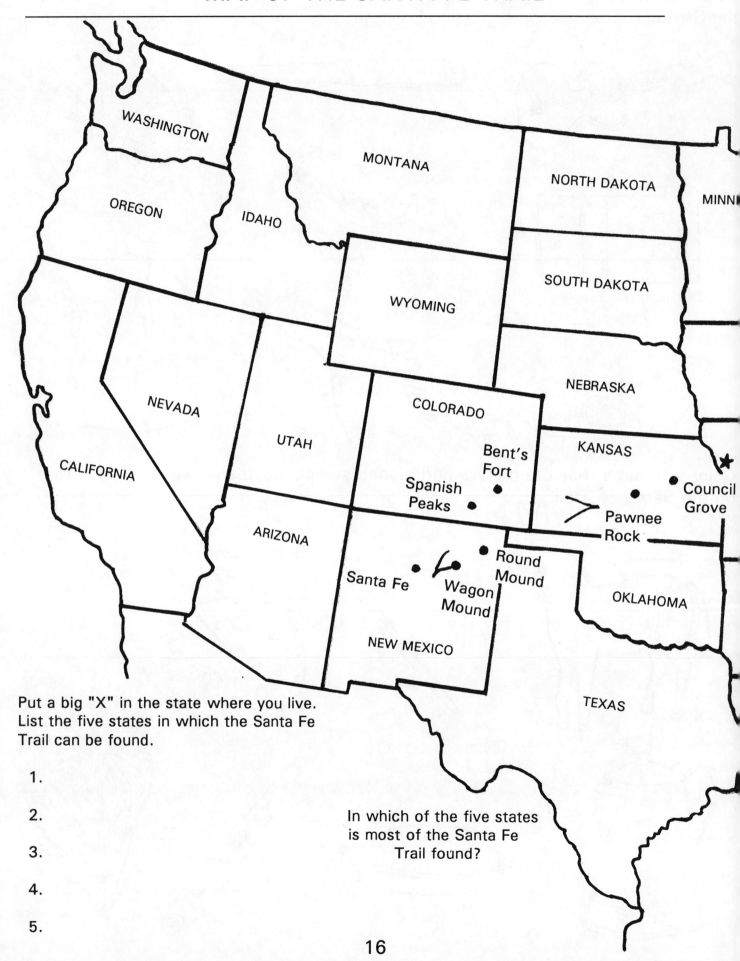

WASHINGTON

MONTANA

NORTH DAKOTA

MINN

OREGON

IDAHO

SOUTH DAKOTA

WYOMING

NEVADA

NEBRASKA

COLORADO

KANSAS

UTAH

CALIFORNIA

Bent's Fort

Spanish Peaks

Council Grove

Pawnee Rock

ARIZONA

Round Mound

Santa Fe

Wagon Mound

OKLAHOMA

NEW MEXICO

TEXAS

Put a big "X" in the state where you live.
List the five states in which the Santa Fe
Trail can be found.

1.

2.

In which of the five states
is most of the Santa Fe
Trail found?

3.

4.

5.

Draw lines to complete the Santa Fe Trail. Start at Independence, Missouri, where the star is. Then connect the dots that represent the places described in the coloring section at the beginning of the book. Some of these places were landmarks. Other places represent cities or forts. NOTE: The Santa Fe Trail split into two parts. The portions of the trail where it divided and re-joined are already drawn.

FOODS

During the early years of the Santa Fe Trail there were no places to stop to buy food. Also, the traders and travelers did not have the ready-made foods that we have today. They had to prepare everything they ate. Some of the foods that they took with them were flour, corn meal, rice, salted pork, and dried fruits. Most of their foods were cooked over a fire. Later, when stagecoaches carried people along the trail they stopped at stage stations and ranches to get their meals. Here are three types of foods used on the trail or in the Southwest. The first is a bread, the second is a main dish, and the third is a dessert.

Be sure to have an adult help you.

CORN BREAD

There is a variety of old corn bread recipes. This one uses baking powder which makes it lighter. Old recipes used saleratus or baking soda. It needed only a few minutes to prepare. Usually it was cooked in a frying pan or baked in a Dutch oven. To make it more easily, bake it in a modern oven.

INGREDIENTS

1 1/2 cups corn meal	1/4 cup sugar	1/2 teaspoon salt
1/2 cup flour	1 egg	(it can be eliminated)
1 tablespoon baking powder	1 cup milk	
(or 1 teaspoon baking soda)	1/4 cup margarine	

1. Combine and mix dry ingredients.

2. Combine milk, egg, and melted margarine.

3. Pour liquid into the dry mixture.
   Stir only enough to moisten the batter.

4. Pour into a 9" X 9" greased baking pan.

5. Bake in an oven for about 20-25 minutes at 400 degrees.

6. Best when served hot with butter.

Dutch oven

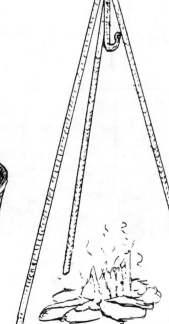

Camp tripod

Spider frying pan / skillet

18

MEXICAN RICE

Rice was brought to Mexico by the Spaniards and it quickly became part of the local diet. Like most Mexican foods, rice dishes are well seasonsed.

INGREDIENTS

2 cups raw rice	1/2 stick butter	2 tablespoons chopped green pepper
3 cups chicken stock	1 clove minced garlic	pinch each of salt & pepper
16 oz. tomato sauce	1/2 cup chopped onions	

1. In half the butter, saute onion, garlic and peppers until onions are golden.

2. Add remaining butter and rice. Cook gently 5 minutes.

3. Stir in tomato sauce and heat thoroughly, then add chicken stock.

4. Cover and cook gently over low heat for about 20 minutes. Salt and pepper to taste.

BREAD PUDDING

Bread pudding is also an old favorite recipe. There are many variations of it.

INGREDIENTS

5 pieces dried or toasted white bread, cubed or broken-up	1 cup brown sugar	1 teaspoon vanilla
	1 teaspoon nutmeg	1/4 cup raisins
3 cups milk, scalded	1 1/2 teaspoon cinnamon	4 oz cream cheese
3 eggs, well beaten	1/4 cup melted butter	1 sliced apple

1. Combine milk and bread in buttered baking dish. Soak for ten minutes.

2. Combine sugar and spices in mixing bowl.

3. Stir in eggs and melted butter. Add the rest of ingredients.

4. Pour over the bread pieces/cubes. Stir lightly.

5. Bake 30 minutes at 350 degrees.

Round bottom kettle

MUSIC

Traders, teamsters, and pioneers often brought along a variety of musical instruments, such as guitars, fiddles, banjos, and harmonicas. In the evenings when they camped after a long hard day they often sang songs for enjoyment and relaxation. "Buffalo Gals" was a popular tune first heard on the trail in the 1840s. Sometimes they added or changed the verses as they traveled. You can too!

As I was walk-in' down the street, Down the street, down the street, A

pret-ty lit-tle girl I chanced to meet, Oh, she was fair to see.

Chorus for vs. 1, 2 & 3

Buf-fa-lo gals, won't you come out to-night? Come out to-night? Come out to-night?

Buf-fa-lo gals, won't you come out to-night? And dance by the light of the moon?

Additional chorus for vs. 3

Oh buf-fa-lo gals, won't you come out to-night, and dance by the light of the moon?

I asked her if she'd have a dance, Have a dance, care to dance.
I thought_ that_ I might get a chance To shake a foot with her.
Chorus

I asked that gal to be my wife, Be my wife, be my wife.
I'd be so ver-y hap-py all my life If she were by my side.
Chorus

Travelers on the Santa Fe Trail had many dangers to overcome.

Find the safe paths for the travelers to take so they avoid the three dangers shown below. Draw a line in each to show the safe route.

Rugged Mountains

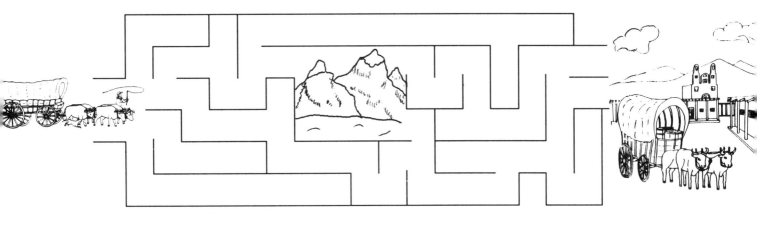

Deserts with no water

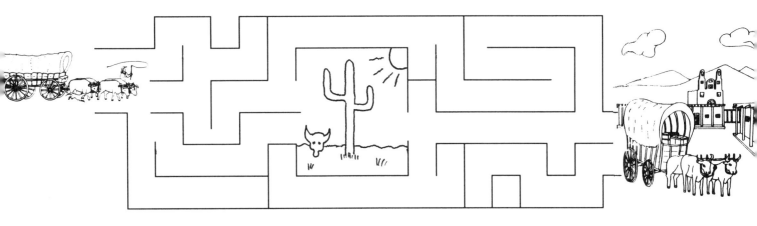

Indian Attacks

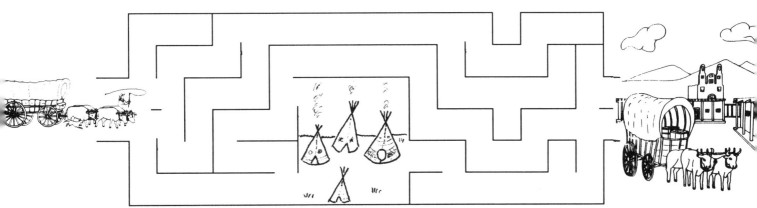

What do you think were some other dangers the travelers faced?

Help the traders and merchants find their way to Santa Fe so they can
  sell their trade goods.
Draw a path for them to follow.
Don't cross over any lines or run into any dangers.

Independence, Missouri (Start here)

Santa Fe

22

Study the top drawing which shows a wagon outside Bent's Fort.
Ten things are missing in the bottom drawing.
Do you know what they are? Add them to the bottom drawing.

23

Two pictures in each row are exactly the same. Circle them.

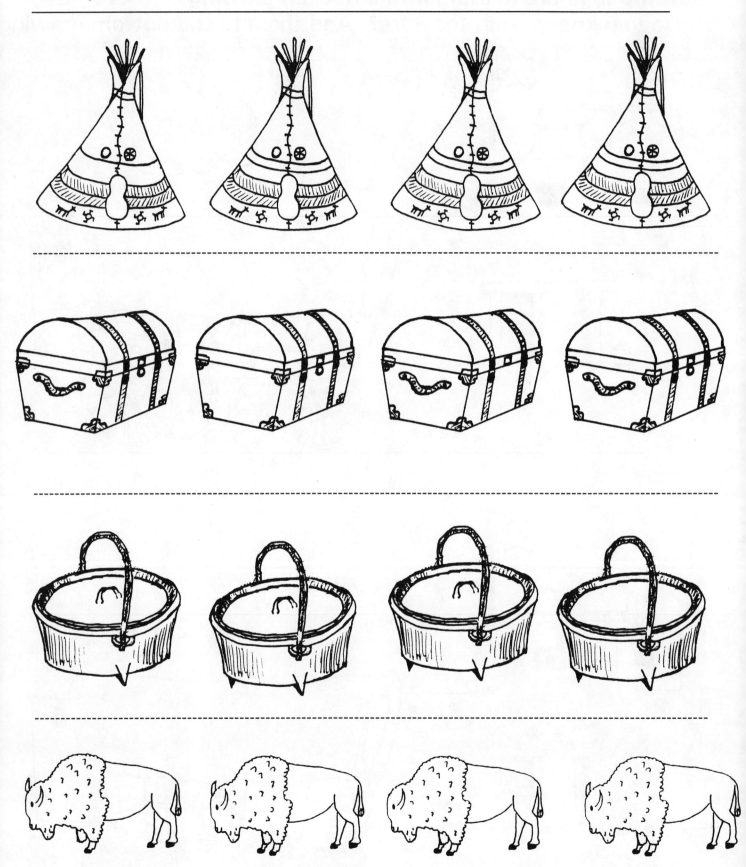

Put an X on the item that doesn't belong in each box.

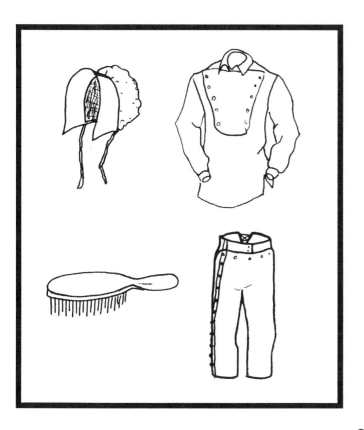

What items go together?

Traders sold dry goods, hardware and notions. Dry goods were clothing and material. Hardware items were tools, and notions were small personal items. Below are different goods the traders sold.
  Color the dry goods red.
  Color the hardware goods blue.
  Color the notions yellow.

How many dry goods did you color?

How many pieces of hardware did you color?

How many notions did you color?

The merchants have lost some of their trade goods while stopping to camp for the night at Point of Rocks in New Mexico. See if you can help them by finding the missing items listed at the bottom of the page. Circle or color them in the picture.

Here are the missing trade items that you are to find in the drawing.

Kettle	Needle	Ax	Hair Brush
Frying Pan	Thread	Hoe	Button
Pot	Butcher Knife	Tacks	Scissors

Can you find it?

Read the story. Then find the words underlined in the story in the puzzle below. Circle the words in the puzzle.

WINDWAGON THOMAS

Crossing the prairie in a covered wagon pulled by oxen was difficult.

A man named William Thomas tried to make it easier. He thought that the prairie looked like an ocean of grass where the wind always blew. He built a wagon that had square sails like a ship. He called it a windwagon. He then hired a crew of men to help him sail the wagon on the prairie just like a ship.

Many people wanted to see the windwagon. On the day of the trip people brought lunches and sat on the prairie to watch it sail.

William and his men put the windwagon on the top of a hill. All of a sudden a big wind came up and filled its sails. The windwagon took off and moved faster and faster.

Members of the crew got scared and jumped off. With nobody to help him sail it, the windwagon crashed into a ditch. No one was hurt. The people who were watching thought it was all very funny!

From then on, William Thomas was called "Windwagon Thomas."

Do you think that the windwagon was a good idea?

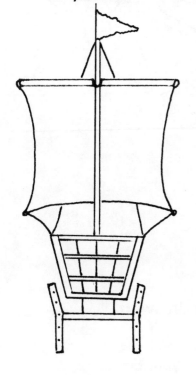

S	H	O	P	R	A	I	R	I	E
H	G	F	E	F	U	N	N	Y	I
I	T	H	O	M	A	S	A	F	D
P	R	X	P	W	O	R	T	O	E
S	A	I	L	S	C	U	R	T	A
N	C	R	E	W	R	H	I	L	L
C	R	A	S	H	E	D	P	M	S
W	I	N	D	W	A	G	O	N	W

 Then and Now

Susan Magoffin was only eighteen years old when she married a trader. She and her husband, Samuel, traveled to Santa Fe on their honeymoon in 1846. She wrote about their adventures in a diary. It was called <u>Down the Santa Fe Trail and into Mexico</u>. Life was different during Susan's time than it is today. Below is a list of experiences. Put a check in front of those things you think Susan could have written about in her diary.

_____1. Stopping at a mall for last minute trip supplies.

_____2. Climbing Pawnee Rock and writing her name on it.

_____3. Having her wagon turn over when going down a steep bank.

_____4. Hearing a coyote howl at night.

_____5. Admiring the beauty of a rainbow after a prairie rainstorm.

_____6. Having the wagon get stuck in the mud.

_____7. Having a tow truck pull her wagon out of the mud.

_____8. Watching the lights of an airplane fly overhead in the clear night sky.

_____9. Stopping and resting at Bent's Fort.

_____10. Taking a can of Coca Cola from the cooler while crossing the hot plains.

_____11. Listening to the radio for the next day's weather report.

_____12. Riding her horse on the prairie.

_____13. Seeing the Spanish Peaks.

_____14. Using her flashlight to see inside her tent at night.

_____15. Learning to speak Spanish.

_____16. Telephoning her parents to let them know they arrived safely in Santa Fe.

_____17. Watching Mexican children at play.

_____ 18. Taking a taxi ride around Santa Fe to see the sights.

Write the word that is described in each sentence in the space below it.
Then write the letters in the spaces in the crossword puzzle.

<table>
<tr><td>DOWN</td><td>ACROSS</td></tr>
<tr><td>1. The city that the
traders wanted to get to

_____</td><td>3. The merchants traded
these in Santa Fe

_____</td></tr>
<tr><td>2. A large grassland

_____</td><td>5. The merchants carried
their goods in it

_____</td></tr>
<tr><td>3. Food that the animals
ate on the prairie

_____</td><td>6. Another word for merchants

_____</td></tr>
<tr><td>4. These animals were used
to pull the wagons

_____</td><td>7. A hot dry area

_____</td></tr>
</table>

HOW TO BUILD BENT'S FORT

Materials and Instructions: (for a smaller fort)

You will only need scissors, scotch tape, toothpick & markers.
Copy the pattern on page 32 on a copying machine.
Then follow instructions 5 through 16 below.

Materials: (for a larger fort)

White or tan construction paper. Piece of 10" x 12" with 1/2" grid or 20" x 24" with 1" grid.
Pencils, ruler, square, scissors, glue or scotch tape
Magic Markers - black or brown, red, & blue
One toothpick or coffee stirrer

Instructions: Ask an adult to help you.

NOTE: by using grids of different sizes or scales you can make the fort as large as you wish.

1. Lay one piece of the construction paper flat. Draw your grid squares very lightly.

2. Use the patterns (I, II. & III) on the next page as your model. First, draw all the heavy solid lines for the outside pattern of the fort (I) on the construction paper. Follow them precisely.

3. Second, draw the dash lines on the pattern. These will later be used for fold lines.

4. Now use the brown or black magic marker to draw all the fort's features on patterns I, II, & III. Be sure to put them in the correct places.

5. Now cut out the pattern by cutting on the solid outside lines. Also, cut along the front tower lines. If you wish, cut the front gate doors so that they open.

6. Cut out the two strips (II) & (III) for the two round corner bastions.

7. Make a fold at all #1 dash lines.

8. Make a fold at all #2 dash lines.

9. Make a fold at all #3 dash lines.

10. Make a fold in the opposite direction on all #4 dash lines.

11. Glue or tape the paper along #4 line folds to the inside bottom of the fort.

12. Take patterns II & III and make two cylinders as shown and place them on the round corner sections. Tape each to the wall section of the fort pattern as shown.

13. Use the flag pattern & markers to make a flag.

14. Cut out the flag pattern.

15. Fold and glue the flag pattern around one end of the toothpick.

16. Tape the toothpick to the inside of the front tower section to complete your fort.

COMPLETED FORT

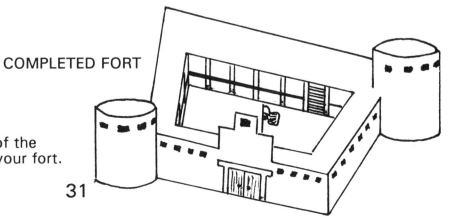

BENT'S FORT PATTERNS

Copy this page directly to make a small fort. To make a larger fort, use the grids to transfer the pattern to your own construction paper. (Note: Using oaktag would make the fort more solid, but it is harder to make precise folds.)

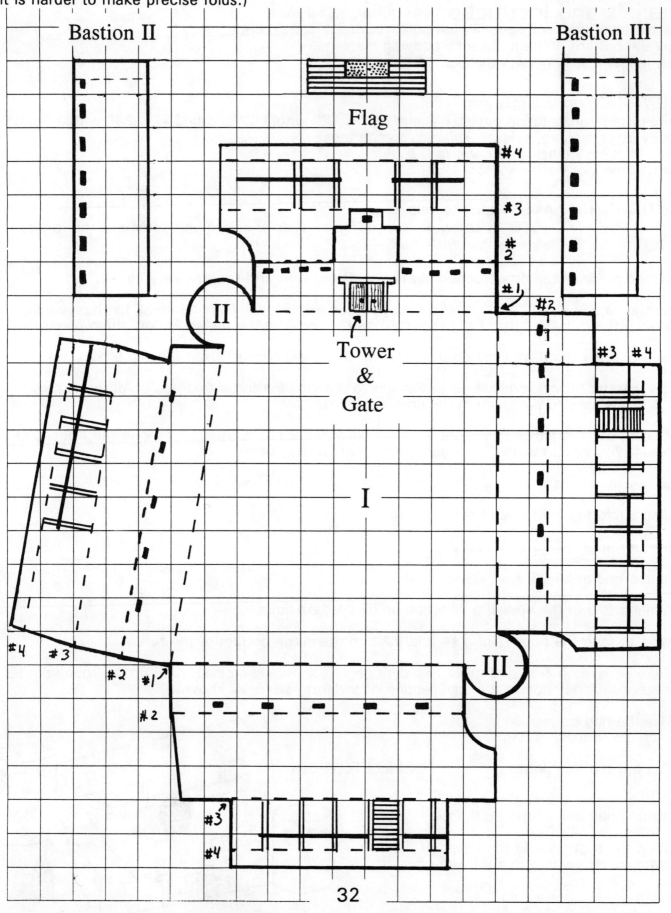

Bastion II

Bastion III

Flag

#4

#3

#2

#1

II

#2

Tower
&
Gate

#3 #4

I

#4 #3

#2 #1

#2

III

#3

#4